Thomas Meyrick

Life of St. Wenefred

Virgin martyr and abbess, patroness of North Wales and Shrewsbury

Thomas Meyrick

Life of St. Wenefred

Virgin martyr and abbess, patroness of North Wales and Shrewsbury

ISBN/EAN: 9783741185298

Manufactured in Europe, USA, Canada, Australia, Japa

Cover: Foto ©Lupo / pixelio.de

Manufactured and distributed by brebook publishing software (www.brebook.com)

Thomas Meyrick

Life of St. Wenefred

By the same Author.

GENELLI'S LIFE OF ST. IGNATIUS. 6s.

SARASA'S ART OF ALWAYS REJOICING. 2s. 6d.

PINAMONTI'S ART OF KNOWING OURSELVES; or, Glass that does not deceive. 2s. 6d.

A LIFE OF ST. WALBURGE, with the Itinerary of St. Willibald. 2s. 6d.

LIFE OF ST. WILLIBRORD. 3s.

LIFE OF ST. WINFRID OR BONIFACIUS. 2s. 6d.

LIFE OF ST. WENEFRED,

Virgin Martyr and Abbess.

PATRONESS OF NORTH WALES AND SHREWSBURY.

BY THE
REV. THOMAS MEYRICK, M.A.,
AUTHOR OF "ST. WILLIBRORD," ETC.

LONDON:
R. WASHBOURNE, 18 PATERNOSTER ROW.
1878.

PREFACE.

The spider which gave comfort to Bruce scarcely attempted oftener to spin its web than the author to publish the life of St. Wenefred. Hitherto the attempt has been disappointed, and it is now made under the disadvantage of the loss of many references collected with much trouble. The reader must, therefore, be content with such general references as are given to Welsh antiquarians, and other authorities.

The sources of the life are, first, two manuscripts of the Cottonian Library of the British Museum—one entitled "Vita B. Wenfredæ, per Elerium Britm. Monachum," the other inscribed "Liber Bibliothecæ Stæ. Mariæ et Stæ. Ethelfledæ virginis, de Romsey." They contain the life by St. Elerius, contemporary of St. Wenefred. Secondly, the life by Robert, monk of Shrewsbury in the time of King Stephen. References are also made to Alford's

Annals, and in the first or introductory chapter John of Glastonbury is quoted, also from the British Museum. The author regrets most the loss of references to the Welsh antiquarians, Lewis, Rees, Thomas, etc.

Doubtless there is much in the life of St. Wenefred which is difficult to believe. Let the incredulous visit the well, and pray there. Let them see for themselves the wonders that are continually worked there by the hand of God.

The miracles of the life of St. Walburga, written by the author of St. Wenefred, provoked at one time the hostility of the incredulous. It has been his misfortune, or good fortune, to write the lives of two saints, each of them miraculous for nearly, or fully, twelve hundred years. That of St. Wenefred has an additional difficulty, that she was restored to life after her martyrdom. She was martyred at Holywell, she died again at Gwytherin. So say all the ancient lives and traditions of St. Wenefred. To deny this is to deny the veracity of her history and of her historians.

If it be not true, how came her body and tomb to be at Gwytherin in the time of King Stephen, when she was translated to Shrewsbury? It may be surmised that the body was carried from Holywell to Gwytherin at some period between 660 and 1100, but of this there is no trace or probability. Neither the people of Holywell nor the monks of Basingwerk would have suffered the body to be removed. Gwytherin is far away, some thirty miles; the paths to it, which the author has traversed, wild and mountainous, and the place comparatively insignificant.

That St. Wenefred was entombed at Gwytherin is certain. From thence the body was translated to Shrewsbury. Of this there is no doubt. Pennant, in his "Tour in Wales," says (vol. ii. page 181), speaking of Gwytherin:

"In the church is shown the box in which her reliques were kept, before their removal to Shrewsbury. Here is also an ancient grave stone, with a flowery cross and chalice. . . .

"The saint's chapel, Capel Gwenfrewi" (or Chapel of St. Wenefred), "is now totally destroyed. It stood on the south side of the church, but nothing remains except some slight ditches and foundations. In this chapel was a tombstone, with a singular cross engraven on it, and by the cross an ancient battleaxe."

A small piece of this box or coffer, which is said to have contained the relics, was obtained by the author on his visit to Gwytherin some twenty-seven years since.

Again, since the tomb and burial-place of the Saint was certainly at Gwytherin, why was Holywell always her place of pilgrimage and of wonderful miracles, except on account of her martyrdom and the well which miraculously arose on the spot?

To those who are unacquainted with the antiquities of Wales, genealogies are spoken of which may seem legendary. But Pennant and Lloyd, Rees, and Thomas, and Lewis are sufficient authorities, and much more corroborative matter could be taken from them, especially in the life of St. Beuno.

The churches still stand, or the localities retain the name of the saints who figure in the brief history of St. Wenefred.

Of these the most important, next perhaps to St. Beuno, is St. Elerius, the contemporary of the Saint and the author of her early life, from which Robert of Shrewsbury drew his materials. A portion of this, containing all the important matter, exists in two manuscripts of the Cottonian Library in the British

Museum. They are not copies of the same manuscript. One purports to be the life by Elerius, the British monk ; the other is a different version, but from the same original source. The Sarum Office contains materially the same account in its lessons, probably compiled from Robert the Prior, of Shrewsbury.

It remains only to add that the frontispiece is a woodcut designed a number of years since by an immediate scholar of Augustus Welby Pugin.

Feast of the Purification,
    1878.

CONTENTS.

CHAPTER	PAGE
I. CHRISTIAN BRITAIN	11
II. STATE OF WALES	18
III. ST. BEUNO	24
IV. ST. WENEFRED	29
V. THE RESUSCITATION	34
VI. DEPARTURE FROM HOLYWELL	39
VII. SECOND DEATH AT GWYTHERIN	45
VIII. TRANSLATION TO SHREWSBURY	50
IX. THE WELL	54
X. LATER MIRACLES	61
XI. THE WELL AT THE PRESENT DAY	68
XII. APPENDIX	72

LIFE OF ST. WENEFRED.

CHAPTER I.

CHRISTIAN BRITAIN.

In the chronicle of John of Glastonbury (Brit. Mus.) we read: "The hand of man made not the Church of Glastonbury, but our Lord Jesus Christ, the Great High-priest, Maker of Heaven and Earth, and Redeemer of Man. It is called by the English, Eald Chirche, or Old Church, and to swear by it is a most solemn oath. For it is the first and oldest church in England, being built of wattle-work of willows, and from it spread the Holy Faith into all the land; and though it was of poor fabric, it was of great reverence, and it is called the *Second Rome.*"

He goes on to say that the isle in which it stands was called Inis-wytrin (*insula vitrea*), the Blue Isle, or Avalon, the Isle of Apples; and the place Glastonbury, or City of the Blue Isle. He gives a long catalogue of the saints buried there, and mentions especially the miraculous crucifix which spoke to the Monk Ailsi—" for he had often past it without an inclination of respect, and when at last one day he made a reverence, a voice came from it, saying, ' Now too late, Ailsi !' and the monk dropped dead;" also the miraculous image of the Blessed Virgin, which arrested the great fire.

The history of St. Joseph of Arimathea is thus given in brief. He was imprisoned in a dungeon by the Jews for having asked of Pilate the body of the Lord. Christ, risen from the dead, released him from prison by a miracle, and conveyed him to Arimathea. He first dwelt with the Blessed Virgin and St. John at Ephesus, and then, in the fifteenth year after the Assumption of the Blessed Virgin, followed St. Philip the Apostle into Gaul, and was sent by him, with twelve companions, into Britain. There, after other adventures and imprisonment, he was favourably received by Arviragus in the west, who, though he did not embrace the Faith, gave him Inis-wytrin ; and, admonished by the angel Gabriel, the twelve built there a church of willow wattle-work, which Christ Himself dedicated to the honour of His Holy Mother, Mary, ever virgin. Joseph was buried there, near the chapel, "at the point where two lines meet" (*lineâ bifurcatâ*). The chronicler adds a strange British prophecy, which runs as follows: "The Isle of Avalon is adorned beyond all others in the world with the sepulchres of prophets, and is hereafter to be renowned. There lies Abbadar the king in Saphat famous of old, with a hundred and four thousand. Amongst whom rests Joseph de Marmore of Arimathea, and he is laid in the bifurcate line near the chapel of the potent adorable Virgin, where the thirteen once dwelt. He has with him in his tomb two white silver vessels, containing sweat and blood of the prophet Jesus. When his tomb shall be found whole and intact, it shall be a place of pilgrimage to all the world. Then the rain and dew of Heaven shall fail no more to the renowned isle. These things shall be notorious to all the world some length of time before the judgment day in the Vale of Josaphat."

A hundred and three years after the coming of St. Joseph to Britain, Lucius the king, the son of Coel, great-grandson of Arviragus, sent to Eleutherius, the thirteenth pope after St. Peter, to ask for doctors of the Faith. Fagan and Divian (Fugatius and Damian) baptised the king, and evangelised Britain. They came to Glastonbury, and found the Cross and the ancient chapel. There they finally took up their abode in that most ancient British monastery. They established in Britain three archbishoprics and eight and twenty bishoprics, corresponding, says Ptolemy, to the three archdruids and twenty-eight chief priests. The three metropolitan sees were Caerleon-upon-Usk, London, and York, according to the chronicle of Robert of Gloucester (Brit. Mus.).

" There were in Englond for false laws to lere
Eight-and-twenty chief studs, bishoprics as it were,
And three architemples as it were highest of each one,
London, and Eurewick, and in Glamorgan one.
This good king he let his holy men selle them all here,
And eight-and-twenty bishoprics in their studes lette rere."

The memory of ancient British Christianity has well-nigh passed away; but from its conversion, A.D. 136, to the landing of the Saxons in 450, Britain was Christian, and another century passed before the last Celtic bishop of London, Theonius, quitted his see to fly before the Saxons. The records of its saints during those primitive ages are lost or forgotten; but in the dreadful persecution of Diocletian it is said there were countless martyrs; that the Christians fled to the dens and caves of the earth. The name of St. Alban remains as the protomartyr recorded by the pen of St. Bede, and St. Julius and Aaron at Caerleon, in the Roman martyrology. With the exception of these, and the saints of Celtic origin connected with the conversion of the Northumbrian Saxons, St. Aidan and St. Cuthbert and a few others, the British saints are without memorial. The names of some few are perpetuated in Wales and Cornwall and Scotland, but amongst them all the most venerable is St. Wenefred, patroness of the diocese of Shrewsbury and of North Wales. Not excepting the great St. David, her name remains the most famous, both on account of the miracles at her well and the extraordinary circumstances of her life and martyrdom, which have scarcely any parallel in ecclesiastical history.

The grand old Celtic character of sanctity derived from its prototype St. Joseph of Arimathea, was chiefly Eremitical or Cœnobite. The worship of the Cross and Passion was a distinctive feature of it, attested by the old crosses with rude characters inscribed still to be seen, as in Valle Crucis, near Llangollen, and elsewhere. The recluses often lived alone, or surrounded by a few others, as the Syrian or Nitrian Anchorites, and in their lonely chapels celebrated the divine mysteries, or recited the whole Psalter of David during the hours of the night, plunged in some cold fountain or river. Such was the custom of St. Kentigern, St. Patrick, and Drithhelm, the monk recorded by St. Bede.

Slowly the Saxon invaders won from its inhabitants the land of Loegrin, the lowlands of England. Step by step, and by desperate battles, they fought their way for more than a hundred and fifty years. They spared none unless they apostatised, and the multitudes of the slain were looked upon as martyrs. Beginning from Kent and the Isle of Thanet, the crews of the sea-dragon ships gradually devoured the old inhabitants. First the Forest of Andredswold, then Hampshire, and next Salisbury Plain was the battlefield. Then came Wansdyke and Berbery Hill, where for once the Britons gained the day with Saxon aid. After this, in the year 614, came the last great conflict in the southern counties, the battle of Bindon, in Dorset, one of the few of which an authentic memory remains. The

British fought, according to their custom, as Roman legionaries, under tribunes and centurions, with spear and buckler and knights in armour, against the Saxon pike or halberd. It is said that the Christian army was terrified at the sight of the burly Saxons with their huge halberds, which swept down man and horse, and their broad double-headed battle-axes gleaming in their belts. With these the last British army was hewn in pieces, and the remnant fled into Devonshire and Cornwall, or retired into the fastnesses of Wales.

In the same manner the kingdom of Ella, in the north, gradually pushed westward, until, in the time of Ethelfrid the Cruel, the year before the battle of Bindon, A.D. 613, the Saxons held the North of Britain from Edinburgh to Anglesea, and Ethelfrid gained his surname from the slaughter of the monks of Bangor, because they prayed for the British army upon the hill above the battlefield.

This brings us to the date of St. Wenefred, who was born at the close of the life and reign of Cadwal, King of Gwyneth, and commander-in-chief of the British princes leagued against the Saxons, to whom Cadvan succeeded, in whose time she was martyred.

CHAPTER II.

STATE OF WALES.

WALES consisted of three principal kingdoms,. —South Wales or Glamorgan, which held the first rank in former times under the renowned Arthur; Gwyneth or North Wales, which now was first in power under Cadwal, successor of Maelgwyn; and Powysland, which comprised Montgomeryshire and part of Denbighshire and the bank of the Severn nearly to Hereford. Besides these there was the kingdom of Brecknock.

Gildas speaks of the state of Christianity as deplorable. He calls the kings or tyrants of his time degenerate and disgraceful. But this must be taken with some exception. Caswallon the Long-haired, or else Maelgwyn, gave to St. Kentigern the lands at St. Asaph for the support of nine hundred monks. Possibly it may have been for homicide with which Maelgwyn is charged by Gildas, and such was the gift of Meuric of Glamorgan for the slaughter of Cuneth at the altar. He gave a large tract of land along the banks of the Severn and the Wye as a mulct to St. Oudoc, as may be seen in the Book of Llandaff. Tewdric, his father, was a saint, and resigned his throne for a hermitage, from which he was called to fight against the Saxons. He stood in his armour to defend the ford of the Wye at Tintern, and there received his death-wound in victory. He was carried to Mathern, near Chepstow, where he was buried and revered as a martyr. Brechin, the holy king of Brecknock, is said to have had twenty daughters accounted saints, one of whom was St. Keyne. St. Beuno alone, the uncle of St. Wenefred, is sufficient to refute the charge of general depravity. Besides, in the life of St. Wenefred, we shall meet with St. Deifer, Elerius, and other contemporary saints.

The charge of Gildas evidently applies to the princes chiefly, such as Maelgwyn, whom he calls an apostate monk; and to them, as compared with former Christian kings. We shall find Cadvan behaving with impiety to St. Beuno, and Caradoc, an impious libertine, a prince of Powysland.

Notwithstanding such exceptions, faith was not dead among the Britons. Their hatred of the persecuting Saxons prevented them from partaking in the work of St. Augustine, who at the time of which we speak had closed his grand mission and earthly career; and had they wished to do so the reciprocal hatred of the Saxons would have given them little scope for action. They were at internecine war, and Bede, who wrote at the close of this century, was cut off from all communication with Wales. There was no probability and scarcely a possibility of his hearing of the name of St Wenefred. But it is so far from being true that there was any difference in the faith of St. Augustine and the faith of the British bishops, that he asked them to join him in the work of conversion, which he could not have done had there been the least difference in faith, and St. Oudoc himself, Bishop of Llandaff, was consecrated at Canterbury. "St Oudoc was sent with his aforesaid clergy, Merchwyn Elward, etc., to the blessed archbishop at the city of Canterbury (Dorobernensem), where he was consecrated bishop of the church of Llandaff founded in honour of St. Peter" (*Liber Landavensis*, p. 372).

Thus all the often-repeated story that the old British Church was hostile to Rome and the preaching of its missioners falls to the ground. The Bishops of Llandaff and others claimed a jurisdiction derived from Rome in long ages past, separate from Canterbury and from St. Augustine, whose mission was to the English. The Churches in Ireland and Scotland, planted by St. Patrick and St. Ninian, did the same, and were not subject to Saxon jurisdiction, except so far as St. Augustine had commission from Rome to correct all abuses in the British Isles.

As an example of the flourishing condition of monastic life in Wales, we may take the history of St. Kentigern mentioned in the last chapter. By the Welsh he is called Cyndeyrn, in Scotland better known as Mwyngu (or Mungo), "the Beloved." He fled from Glasgow and Dumfriesshire, where the people had apostatised, leaving the vale of the Clyde in Scotland for the vale of the Clwyd in Wales. He received lands from the king of North Wales and established a monastery of nine hundred monks, six hundred choir monks, and three hundred lay brothers. This was in the middle of the sixth century, and he remained about twenty years, leaving St. Asaph his successor in Wales. St. Asaph was chosen by a miracle. The Abbot Kentigern reciting the nocturns in the icy river according to custom, was frozen with cold, and desired Asaph, his monk, to bring him fire from a neighbouring house. The churlish householder bade the monk, who had no vessel to receive the lighted charcoal, to carry it in his bosom. St. Asaph carried the coals to his master in his habit, which was not singed by the fire.

St. Kentigern returned to Glasgow, invited by Roderic, the king. On his return to Galloway, then the province of Valentia, he worked a great miracle deserving of record. Roderic, who wished to restore the faith, met him with the repentant apostate people, who had gone back to the gods of the Walhalla. St. Kentigern bid them kneel and pray while he made over them the sign of the Cross, and then lift up their eyes. They saw the phantom forms of the demons forsaking them borne away upon the clouds in the air.

It was the custom of the British from the time of the Romans to elect an emperor or Gwledig (*Dux populi*), the commander-in-chief of the princes and people of Britain. This was afterwards continued by the Saxons in the Bretwalda, the lord of Britain.

Cadwal was commander-in-chief at the time

of the battle of Chester, where he was slain with many of the princes of Wales by Ethelfred the Cruel in the year 613, and was succeeded by Cadvan, king also of Gwyneth, whose residence was at Caernarvon.

This powerful prince was enabled as commander-in-chief to gather a very large army or host, apparently both from South Wales and Cornwall and the middle shires of England, where the old heathen Penda for a long time assisted the British against the Northumbrian king. Cadvan beat back the Saxons from Chester and advanced as far as Dilston in Northumbria, where, slain in battle by St. Oswald, then king, he perished, with the flower of the British army, in the year 635.

This date more or less ascertains that of St. Wenefred. St. Beuno, after the martyrdom of St. Wenefred, leaving Holywell, went to the court of Cadvan, at Caernarvon, then in the plenitude of his power, to apply for some land, as in the sequel will be narrated, and she could not have been much less than fifteen, or perhaps fourteen, at the time of her martyrdom. St. Wenefred must, therefore, have been born early in the seventh century, at some time before the year 620.

CHAPTER III.

ST. BEUNO.

THE history of St. Beuno is so interwoven with that of St. Wenefred, that no apology is needed for this chapter. This great saint was born in Montgomeryshire, near the spot where the river Rhyw falls into the Severn. He was an only son, born in his parents' old age. His mother is said to have been the daughter of Anna, sister of Arthur. Hence he is called uncle of St. Wenefred, whose mother was of the same noble race. The child was educated by a holy abbot or monk, in Latin called Dangesius, and embraced the monastic life. Having closed the eyes of his aged father, whom he assisted on his deathbed, he received an invitation from the king of Powysland to found a monastery near Corwen. The late king of Powys had been slain in the battle of Chester, with Cadwal Wledig, and his son, as it would appear, wished to establish a monastery to pray for the soul of his father.

St. Beuno was an Apostle. His progress

may be traced by churches which he founded through all Powysland, until he finally settled his abode at Clynog Vawr, in Caernarvonshire, where he died. Having accepted the offer of the king of Powys, he established a monastic house in the neighbourhood of Corwen, and there his memory is perpetuated by the name of the Irishman's Bog (Gwyddelgwyrn), where he raised a dead Irishman to life.

Whilst he dwelt there, some young men, princes of Powys, came hunting in the neighbourhood of the monastery, and insisted on being entertained by the abbot. St. Beuno must supply them with cooking and food after their hunting. There was nothing unusual in this; in fact, we find it the common custom in after times for the kings and barons to require hospitality of the abbots so long as it pleased them to rest on their journeys and feed upon the monks. St. Beuno provided accordingly, but as it seems they were insolent young men, he put some beef to boil, made the sign of the cross over it, and the water would not cook the meat. Three days and nights the young hunters sat heaping fuel round the pot; but the meat remained raw, it would not cook. They then said in anger, "Let us go, this man is a magician," and they departed. It is not improbable that one of these young princes was Caradoc, who came, not long after this, hunting to Holywell.

Whether it was on account of this circumstance, or for some other reason, St. Beuno shortly afterwards quitted Powysland, and crossed the border which runs over Moel Vamma, by Mold to the Dee, into Gwyneth, to his kinsman Tevith, living in that portion of Wales which was called Tegengle, in the Latin Tekenglia, the strip of lowland lying along the sea coast of Flintshire in which Holywell is situated. It belonged to Gwyneth, but was subject to incursions from Chester, and was possibly a debatable land between Powys and Gwyneth.

Here Tevith, probably a form of David, possessed three prœdia, or estates. The names of these are given in the life of St. Wenefred, by St. Elerius, or Hilary, in the Latin manuscript of the Cottonian Library in the British Museum—the first Abelatye, the second Maengwyn, the third Gwenfynnan. He is styled a brave soldier, son of Eylud, the second in power next the king. This implies no little dignity, as Cadvan was commander-in-chief of all the British princes.

When St. Beuno came to him, Tevith applied for leave to the king to give him land for a church. From this it appears that there was a jealousy on the part of princes in permitting lands to be alienated to the Church, perhaps on account of the loss of military service. The king gave permission, with the proviso that one farm should be given. Tevith gave St. Beuno his choice, and he fixed upon the dry hollow then called Sechnant, and now, from the spring, Holywell, in the solitude of Belatye, or Abelatyc, at the foot of the hill on which the present town stands, where, says Lewis, in his Topographical Dictionary, "there are two fields still called Gerddi St. Beuno, or St. Beuno's Gardens."

Here St. Beuno built a chapel and a cell, and said Mass. Between the Chapel of the Well and Gerddi St. Beuno, there is a well called St. Beuno's Well.

It was the custom in early times, not only for men, but for women, to live as recluses alone. It long prevailed in some parts of Italy, as we find in the life of St. Clare of Montefalco. To become a recluse did not imply as a consequence a monastic house or community; but others, following the example, settled round an anchorite. They met for Mass at least on holidays. Such was the custom of the monks of St. Saba in the Holy Land in the eighth century, and that of the Christian communities in Egypt, described by Philo in the earliest time, we shall find the custom of females living in this manner as separate recluses, forbidden in a Welsh Synod in the life of St. Wenefred.

CHAPTER IV.

ST. WENEFRED.

The daughter of Tevith and Wenlo was an only child. The name of Wenefred was, in all probability, Guenevrea, as she is called in the early lives the Fair or Holy Brea. The Saxon termination of "freda" has given rise to the objection that she was not a British saint at all, if she ever existed. The best way to answer such difficulties is to pass them over with contempt. The defence of the lives of the saints and of their miracles often does much to raise doubts and increase difficulty. Ignorance of true history or malice are best answered by mere statement of truth and documents which support it. Comment is often the ruin of history. Ancient chroniclers seldom waste their time and their readers' patience by philosophising upon the facts they record.

The young and beautiful girl was a devoted listener to St. Beuno, and soon secretly resolved to give herself to God. She was afraid to tell her wishes to her father and mother, but communicated them to St. Beuno. He broke it, at her request, to her parents, and they were neither surprised nor displeased, only she was as yet too young to be allowed to enter into an irrevocable engagement.

Meanwhile, she waited to ratify her resolution, when on a certain Sunday, as the ancient manuscript of Elerius relates, her father and mother having already gone down to Mass at the chapel of St. Beuno, she remained behind to bring fire and water and salt, things wanted for the Mass (*necessaria*). A young stranger prince on a hunting expedition rode up to the house. He was a stranger, for he did not know the name of the possessor of the estate. His name was Caradoc, and he is called the son of Alauc, not Alan, as has been commonly given by an error of transcribers. In the old manuscript it is Alauc, " the son of Alauc of royal race ;" it does not say the king's son, but probably he was the nephew of the king of Powys, one of the young men mentioned above in the life of St. Beuno who are styled nephews of the king. His hunting, and on the Lord's Day, seem to imply a character quite apiece with the anecdote of the young huntsmen at Corwen ; and, as appears in the sequel, he was a former acquaintance of St. Beuno, though a stranger in Tegengle. He had come hunting across the borders of Powysland into Gwyneth and Tegengle, which was liable to such incursions from its neighbours and was far away from Caernarvon.

He was, probably, known at least by name to Wenefred, who excused herself as not fit to appear in her humble dress in presence of a prince. He laughed at her plea of being dedicated to God as a nun by promise, but, persuaded that she was content to accede to the offer of a prince of Powys, he permitted her to go to her chamber to change her dress. She then escaped by a back way, and fled down the valley towards the cell and chapel of St. Beuno.

Caradoc mounted his horse, and pursued. She had gained the door of the chapel when he caught her. Furious at his disappointment, and finding her deaf to his remonstrances, he struck a blow with his sword which severed her head from her body.

St. Beuno came forth from the chapel, where he was preparing for Mass, and, recognising the murderer, reproached him with his cruelty done to one equal to him in birth, and pronounced upon him the Church's malediction.

Caradoc, according to the words of the manuscript ("*liquefactus est*") melted away; according to popular language, was carried off by the devil to hell, or swallowed alive by the earth; in Scriptural phrase, the earth opened its mouth and swallowed him—he went down alive into the pit. There is a similar instance in ecclesiastical history of Drahomira, the incestuous mother of the sainted Duke of Bohemia, Wenceslaus, who procured the murder of her son; and the earth, as is said in the lesson of the saint on the 28th of September, "swallowed her alive."

The earth stained by the blood of Wenefred, in the words of the manuscript, broke asunder, and a fountain burst forth. St. Beuno, taking the head in his hands, placed it with the body beneath his cloak, having breathed into the nostrils. He then explained to the people that the virgin martyr had engaged herself by vow to receive the veil of a religious, and begged them to pray that God would restore her to life to fulfil it. He prayed " that the blessed soul might return to inhabit the body, and, for the sake of the good of souls and the glory of God, sole master of souls and bodies, might live for a long space in this world."

To die a martyr to God in defence of chastity entitled Wenefred to the reward of a blessed saint, and her restoration to life would imply a beatified existence upon earth so far as is compatible with a continuance in the flesh. She would be, in some sense, a living saint canonised by a stupendous miracle. It is obvious that such an example is difficult in its nature. It is the sneer of Gibbon that the stroke of the sword put an end to the miraculous resuscitations of the early martyrs.

Still, that such a favour was granted to the prayers of St. Beuno and the merits of the chaste and holy girl is the unanimous tradition of all the lives and records of St. Wenefred—of St. Elerius, who wrote her life, and saw her and lived with her so many years after her resuscitation; of the localities connected with her in her later years—in fact, of her whole history, as given in the lessons of her Office in the Rite of Sarum.

CHAPTER V.

THE RESUSCITATION.

AFTER the Mass Wenefred arose, wiping off the sweat and blood, as if from a gentle sleep. The head was reunited to the body, but a white circle remained around the neck during her life, and was visible as her distinctive mark in the visions seen of her after her second death.

"If Christ be not risen," says St. Paul, "your faith is vain." The Catholic Faith is built on the resurrection from the dead. Those whom Christ raised from the dead lived many years to attest His power and the truth of the future resurrection. Their living testimony is appealed to long after by a Christian apologist. Instances are given by St. Bede of resuscitation, as that of the monk Drithelmus, who was dead for three days. It is a prelude of the great final resurrection and restoration of all things, and we may hope a figure of the restoration and resurrection of the Faith long discarded in England, and to the majority of its people dead and buried.

Such an extraordinary miracle may be the reason why of so many British saints the memory of St. Wenefred has almost alone remained. She died in defence of chastity, she lived again to attest the resurrection, a point of faith which must be pressed the more as the last days come on when the whole world, as in the days of Noe, will give itself to feasting and merrymaking, and say, " Since our fathers slept all things continue as they were, and there are no signs of the world ending for ever."

The well which arose is equally extraordinary. There is scarcely such another in the world, except the fount of the Jordan, for volume and purity of water. The miracles obtained at it have never ceased; the stones or pebbles of it, which in early times are said to have danced up and down in the well, are still streaked as if with blood.

St. Wenefred now fulfilled her promise, and dedicated her virginity to God as a recluse by vows. She seems to have lived in an ecstatic state of continual communication with our Lord, and to have been regarded as a living martyr. She was still a traveller, but in some sense a *comprehensor*, that is, endowed with the gifts of those who have spiritually risen from the dead.

St. Beuno's work at Holywell was accomplished. He has perpetuated his name as the resuscitator of St. Wenefred. After a short lapse of time he prepared to leave her, and said in prophecy :

"Know that you shall not end your days here, but, after seven years spent in prayer and austerity in this place, to your own great merit and the singular edification of others, our gracious Lord will call you elsewhere, that strangers also may be illuminated by you in His true knowledge and service ; and know also that your memory shall become glorious in future ages, and your merits published to the whole world by miraculous cures and help afforded to the sickly or distressed in mind, who shall pray to you for aid."

Then, seeing her greatly grieved at his departure, he took her by the hand and led her to the well, where sitting upon a stone by its side, which is now in the outer well and is called St. Beuno's stone, he said, as related chiefly by Robert the Prior, and confirmed in the ancient manuscripts :

"You see this monument of your suffering, and the stones stained as if with your blood shed for the sake of your heavenly Spouse. Hear then three special things by which your glorious Spouse and Lord Jesus Christ will honour you and benefit others hereafter by you:

"First. These stones shall never be washed from their stains, but retain them for ever in memorial of your blood shed in a manner so pleasing to Him in defence of your chastity.

"Secondly. No one shall ever devoutly ask any blessing or deliverance from corporal or spiritual distress in this place through your merits and prayers, but that in three times so doing they shall most surely obtain their desire, or else when they pass by death into a better world they shall reap in a more ample manner the fruit of their prayer in heavenly blessings prepared for them through your intercession.

"Thirdly. After my departure from you, which I am about to take, to a distant part of this land, God will give me a cell by the seashore, and when you would send a message or token to me (as His Divine Majesty would have you do, and I entreat of you the same, once a year), cast it into this well or the stream which flows from it, and, passing into the ocean, it will be miraculously conveyed safely to me through many winding shores.

"And these graces shall be told to your renown to the world's end. Stupendous miracles shall be done in this place for the temporal and eternal good of many resorting to it, and even the brute creation shall not want their share in these benefits."

St. Beuno then, bidding her farewell, hastened his pace that she might not follow him, and departed from Holywell.

CHAPTER VI.

DEPARTURE FROM HOLYWELL.

St. Beuno received a gift from the king of Powys of a sceptre of gold. It seems not unlikely that this present, which was of very considerable value, the price of seventy kine, was made as a deodand for the crime committed by Caradoc. The saint presented it to king Cadvan, to whom it would be acceptable to aid him in the expense of his armaments, preparing, as he was, for his great and last expedition into Northumberland, and, perhaps, still more as coming from the king of Powysland, a rival in power. St. Beuno asked the king for land to build a monastery in Gwyneth. Cadvan acceded to his request, both on account of the present and, it is said, also on account of the miracle of the resuscitation of St. Wenefred, which was noised abroad. But Cadvan's gift was like that of King John at Bury, when he gave to the altar a piece of cloth of gold out of the sacristy for which he did not pay. It was land which belonged to a widow and her son. St. Beuno, informed of this, went, accompanied by the widow to the court at Caernarvon, where he found the king surrounded by his princes, and reproached him to his face for his sacrilegious gift, bidding him restore the land to the widow and give him other lands according to his promise. The infatuated king answered the saint rudely, and refused his application, upon which the saint, grieved and in anger, prophesied his future calamity, and was about to pronounce the ban of the Church upon him when he was led aside by one of the nobles, a relative of Cadvan, who persuaded him to be pacified and accept at his hands the estate of Clynog Vaur, and there St. Beuno built his church and monastery, which retains his name.

There he lived and died, and there again raised a dead man to life. He is also said to have gone from thence to Rome, and returned again. Each year St. Wenefred, on the vigil of St. John Baptist, sent her present down the stream, which, passing through the Menai, came ashore near Clynog, at a creek eight miles from Caernarvon; and if popular tradition is to be received, it was named from the coming of the vestment, Porth y Casseg, the

Port of the Chasuble. The history of St. Wenefred was formerly represented on the glass, now broken, at Clynog Church.

After seven years, St. Wenefred received intimation of the death of St. Beuno, and of the Will of God that she should leave Holywell. According to the manuscript of St. Elerius, a council of bishops and abbots was held, at which St. Wenefred was present, and amongst other resolutions it was decreed that virgins should not dwell as recluses apart, but live in communities under monastic rule. This may have been the reason why she left Holywell for the convent at Gwytherin. According to the popular account, St. Wenefred was already abbess of a community at Holywell, and therefore as an abbess would attend the council. This may have been so, or she may have been a recluse surrounded by others under her direction and example. One companion is spoken of as accompanying her pilgrimage.

She seems to have acted under inspired direction, and took her way to Bodvari, about eight miles distant from Holywell. It is said to be so called from the abode of Varus, the Roman emperor, and is situated in the gorge where a little river comes into the Vale of Clwyd from the direction of Mold, at the foot of Mount Arthur, the highest, except Moel Vamma, of the range which closes in to the north-east of that beautiful vale. Here she found St. Diheufar —in Latin, Deifer—whose well, formerly miraculous, and until of late (it is now obstructed by a railroad) revered by the people, was once to be seen. He was of the royal race of Gwyneth, and had three brothers, and uncles to the number of five or six, recognised as saints. Amongst these last was St. Tudno, from whom Llandudno derives its name. The names of the others are recorded by Welsh antiquarians, but except for the purpose of verifying the history of St. Wenefred need not be mentioned here. The reader may be referred to Lewis's "Topographical Dictionary," and others who give the pedigrees of Welsh descents. (See the Appendix.)

By St. Deifer she was received with hospitality, and directed the next day by heavenly inspiration to proceed across the vale to Henllan, the abode of St. Sadwrn or Saturnus. From him, according to the popular account, she received notice from Heaven that Gwytherin in the mountains of Denbighshire was the place appointed for her future dwelling.

He sent a deacon with her to guide her through the wild hills, which like a sea of mountains cover this part of Wales, to the monastery of St. Elerius or Hilary, situated on the beautiful river, said to be called from him the Elwy, not far from Gwytherin, which is upon the Cledwyn, a stream falling into the Elwy.

St. Hilary or Elerius had been a monk at St. Asaph's. He had studied abroad, and had lived some years at Boulogne. He was of royal descent from Maximus Wledig, called the usurper or tyrant, who resisted successfully the arms of Rome. He was related to St. Wenefred, and probably knew well her history. He became her biographer, and his Latin life of her, as may be seen in the portions of it to be found in the manuscripts preserved in the Cottonian Library of the British Museum, may be compared with advantage with the Saxon writers of the time. It is more terse and classical. From him the facts given above are derived, and the same source supplied Robert of Shrewsbury with his more diffuse narrative.

By Elerius, St. Wenefred was conducted to Gwytherin, where his mother, Theonia, an aged abbess, presided over a community of nuns. His words in placing Wenefred among them imply that she was acknowledged as a living Saint: "She is come to die a blessed death among you, having already a high place reserved for her among the most glorious martyrs in heaven."

CHAPTER VII.

SECOND DEATH AT GWYTHERIN.

GWYTHERIN or Witheriacum is a most retired spot in the scattered sea of mountains of Denbighshire, to the south of the Vale of Clwyd. It is still almost untrodden by the foot of the Saxon stranger. Some twelve miles distant, as the crow flies, across the Conway and the Vale of Llanrwst, rises Snowdon with its peaks and attendant chain of mountains.

Here she lived in obedience to the Mother Theonia, regarded with veneration by all, and bearing on her neck the white circle round it, the evidence of her martyrdom. She seems to have been novice-mistress, and in her exhortations she often spoke of the happiness of a blessed death, which is the gate of heaven. On one occasion, when St. Elerius spoke of his hope that she would assist him at his last passage, she replied:

"No, father, it will not be so; Christ has appointed otherwise. You will live to bury the Mother Theonia, and after some few years to bury me, and you will then live some time before you pass into a blessed eternity."

Soon after this Theonia, mother of Elerius, died in odour of sanctity, and Wenefred succeeded to the government of the nuns of Gwytherin. Her prayer was perpetual, and she lived in almost continual ecstasy and communion with Christ, her heavenly Spouse. The discourses she gave to the nuns breathed of the love of Jesus and of virginity. She had a special gift of relieving the mind from temptations and interior distress, of fears and scruples. She was forewarned of her departure by Christ Himself, and communicated the intelligence to St. Elerius. That she might suffer a second martyrdom, her last sickness began with frequent and violent convulsions, which she bore with the sweetest patience, being overjoyed at the approach of death. She only prayed that the devil might not be allowed to disturb or affright her in her last passage. She then addressed the weeping nuns:

"Doubt not, dear children, that in heaven, where by God's grace I am going, I shall do more for you than I can do here on earth by my presence with you; for that promised land is not a place of ignorance, but of clear knowledge, where the blessed understand the wants of their friends on earth, and united with the Fountain-head of infinite charity, they have power to give help, and goodwill to succour them. I promise to do this for you in the kingdom of God. Do not be sad, like those that have no hope. To the children of earth who die in their sins, and dread the coming of the Judge, Death is like an executioner to drag them to the block ; but to pure and innocent souls he is a welcome guest, and he finds them joyful at receiving his embrace, and ready to go at his summons, as those who expect their Lord returning from the wedding."

To the younger nuns she said : " Remember that your bodies, beautiful in their prime, are only prisons of the immortal soul. Take heed to keep them undefiled, and never to forget that the joy of a pure soul on its death-bed recompenses a hundredfold the pleasures it has despised for the love and service of Jesus Christ."

She begged of St. Elerius, from whom she received the last rites of the Church, that her body might be laid beside that of Theonia, and she breathed out her pure soul in an act of intense love into the hands of her Creator and

Redeemer on the vigil of St. John Baptist, as we find in the manuscript inscribed "Book of the Library of St. Mary and Ethelflede, virgin, of Romsey," and was buried "octavo kalendas Julii." (Cotton. Lib., Brit. Mus.)

The vigil of St. John Baptist, the 23rd of June, was the day on which she was wont to send her yearly present to St. Beuno. We may conclude that it was the day of her first martyrdom, as it was also the day of her final departure. This time was kept also as the chief pilgrimage at midsummer to the well. The 3rd of November will have been the feast of her translation to Shrewsbury. Two feasts were kept in her honour in former times: one at midsummer, in June, and another in November; and her Mass, partly that of virgin, and partly virgin and martyr, represents her first and second death.

Her body was laid by that of Theonia, with other saints buried at Gwytherin, amongst whom were St. Chybius, or Gubi, the apostle of Anglesea, from whom Holyhead (Caer Cubi) is named, a disciple of St. Hilary of Poitiers, and St. Sennan, who is probably the same as St. Seiriol, brother of the king, St. Einion, the founder of the monastery, Enlli, or Bardsey Isle. (See Appendix.)

The date of her death is given by Alford as 660, but this is also the date given of St. Elerius' death, who lived some years after her; and we shall be near the truth if we place her birth between the years 610 and 620, and her death, about the age of forty more or less, between 650 and 660.

CHAPTER VIII.

TRANSLATION TO SHREWSBURY.

ST. WENEFRED lay at Gwytherin nearly five hundred years, from the year 650—60 to the reign of King Stephen, A.D. 1138.

In the reign of William the Conqueror, Roger, Earl of Shrewsbury, built a noble monastery in that city, and an abbey church. Relics were wanted for the consecration of the new church, and while the monks were deliberating how to obtain the relics of some great saint, one of the community fell sick and was at the same time afflicted with a deep despondency. Prayers were offered for him both in Shrewsbury and Chester Abbey. The sub-prior of Chester, a man of known sanctity, fell into a trance after prayer, and St. Wenefred appeared to him with the white scar round her neck, and said:

"Let Mass be said for the sick man in my chapel at the well, and he shall recover."

Ralph, the sub-prior, awoke from his trance, but feared that the vision would find no credit, and kept it secret. At last, pity for the sick man, whose distemper increased, obliged him to disclose it. Consultation was held, and it was decided to depute two monks to go to the well and say Mass at the chapel there. At the hour the Mass was said the monk of Shrewsbury recovered.

Upon this it was determined to obtain, if possible, the relics of St. Wenefred for the church in Shrewsbury. Negotiations were begun in the reign of Henry I., but the matter was not effected until the second year of Stephen. Letters were obtained from the Bishop of Bangor, in whose diocese Gwytherin then was, and the promise of aid from a prince of Powys. The two priors of Chester and Shrewsbury went in deputation with five others.

Upon their approach to Gwytherin, they heard that the inhabitants of the country had resolved to oppose their purpose. An apparition of St. Wenefred to one of the party encouraged them to proceed. On the eve of the preceding Easter, the parish priest of Gwytherin was awakened by an angel before the hour of matins, and when he fell asleep, aroused a second and a third time. The angel then bid him rise and follow him to the church. There, pointing to the sepulchre of St. Wenefred, he said :

"Note this place, and my words. I command thee that when some months hence there come men to open this sepulchre and take the body, thou hinder them not, but assist them. Beware of doing otherwise, lest thou suffer for thy disobedience."

The priest, obedient to this heavenly admonition, upon the arrival of the deputation six months after, declared his vision to the people and appeased them. The opposition was thus removed, the sepulchre was opened, and the body removed and carried to Shrewsbury, A.D. 1138.

Herbert was abbot, and Robert the prior. Robert went to Gwytherin to translate the relics. He became the biographer of St. Wenefred, taking his history from the traditions he gathered and from the life of St. Elerius.

The body was received at Shrewsbury with great rejoicings and ringing of the bells. It was placed in St. Giles' Church outside the walls until a shrine was prepared for it in the Abbey Church. At St. Giles's Church, while the relics were exposed there, a complete cripple, whose feet were contracted and his head bowed to his knees, was perfectly cured. As soon as the shrine was ready, the body was carried in solemn procession into Shrewsbury, and while heavy rain fell all around, none fell on the procession as it passed along. Many more miracles recorded by the prior occurred at the entrance of the body into Shrewsbury.

There it lay until the Reformation scattered to the winds the relics of the saints; but the man who broke with a pickaxe into the shrine of St. Wenefred at Shrewsbury not long after broke his own leg, and died miserably.

CHAPTER IX.

THE WELL.

IN very early times astonishing miracles are recorded in the old manuscripts as frequent at the well. The body of a dead girl placed in the well is said to have been resuscitated (Cott. MS. Brit. Mus.). A carpenter's daughter, who was born blind, requested to be carried to the well. She bathed her head in the water, bandaged her eyes, and went to sleep in the chapel. She awoke with sight; and this miracle, which was much noised abroad, led to the founding of the Abbey of Basingwerk.

The messenger of a Welsh prince, sent to warn the country of a Saxon inroad, tied his horse by the chapel at the well as he entered to pray. A thief stole the horse, but his arm with which he seized it swelled and mortified, and he returned to the chapel to restore the beast he had taken and do penance.

Robert of Shrewsbury records a miracle which, he says, caused much fear and reverence among the neighbouring people. A cow stolen from the convent pastures was driven by the robbers over a rocky path, that it might leave no footprints. The feet sank into the road, and left their prints upon the rock. The well, he says, became so famous that mothers cast their sick children into the stream, and they were cured. The blind, the lepers, and the lame were healed, and the register of the cures would require volumes to record them.

Gwytherin as well as Holywell was a place of pilgrimage. An oak-tree near the church-door gave shelter to the pilgrims. A labourer attempted to cut away a bough for his own use, but the hatchet sunk into the wood, while his hand cleaved to the hatchet and remained immovable until, by prayer to St. Wenefred, he obtained his release. The stroke of the hatchet on the bough was shown to Robert of Shrewsbury at his visit to Gwytherin.

After the cure of the monk of Shrewsbury and other miracles, an abbey was built at Basingwerk, which became a preceptory of the Templars in the year 1312. The Knights Templars were placed there by King Henry II. to keep the Welsh Marches. It is a singular case of the employment of that great military order, if, indeed, it was for the purpose of repression;

for Welsh knights were to be found as well as English and Norman among the Crusaders.

After the repression of the Templars, Basingwerk became a Cistercian abbey, and received gifts and charters from the Welsh princes. The miracles at the well were then more carefully recorded, and are celebrated in the following hymn from the Sarum Office:

> " Maid as fair as blooming rose,
>   Virgin, of the Lamb the spouse,
>   Martyr, pure as driven snows
>   Florished Wenefride.
>
> " Born of royal British race,
>   Firm of faith, and bright of face,
>   Living Saint, her soul in grace
>   Free from stain of pride.
>
> " Her the fell Carădoc slew—
>   Hurled to Hell from mortal view,
>   Where, whilst demons have their due,
>   Sinners suffer pain.
>
> " As proof of such a wondrous thing,
>   Raised by God, a rushing spring
>   Stones with stains of blood doth fling
>   Where the maid was slain.
>
> " Multitudes the fountain seek,
>   The blind to see, the dumb to speak,
>   Health is granted to the weak
>   By the prayer of faith.
>
> " Great and glorious Wenefride,
>   Still the swollen billow's tide,
>   Save us from the sin of pride,
>   Be our help in death."

Innumerable miracles continued to be witnessed and recorded down to the change of religion in England. The last Catholic Bishop of St. Asaph, who sat in the Council of Trent, a confessor of the Faith, attested to Baronius, the writer of the Annals, the greatness and number of the miracles at St. Wenefred's Well in his time, which he had witnessed. The saintly Thomas Goldwell, the only English bishop at the Council of Trent, is indeed a worthy witness to the glory of St. Wenefred.

In the persecuting times that followed, particular watch was kept at the well to note the gatherings of the Catholic gentry going in pilgrimage to St. Wenefred.

In the State Papers of the Record Office, A.D. 1623, we find: "Sir Everard Digby confesses to the journey to St. Wenefrid's Well with Darcy (Father Garnet) and Fisher (Father Percy), the whole company thirty horse."—*Montacute Papers.*

A paper endorsed "A Note of Papists and Priests Assembled at St. Wenefrid's Well on St. Wenefrid's Day, A.D. 1629," contains the following long list:

"The Lord William Howard, the Lord of Shrewsbury, Sir Thomas Gerard, Sir William

Norris, Sir Cuthbert Clifton, Mr. Preston of the Manor, Mr. Anderdon of Lostock, Mr. Westley of Westley, Mr. Anderdon of Clerton, Mr. Anderdon of Fourde, Mr. Gerard of Ince, Mr. Bradshawe of Haye, Mr. Harrington of Hightonhye, Mr. Blundell of Crosby, Mr. Scarisbrick of Scarisbrick, Sir John Talbot of Bashaw, Mr. Lathom of Masborough and his five brothers, who are all priests; the Lady Falkland, and with her Mr. Everard the priest; Mr. Price, Mr. Cleiton, priests, with divers other knights, ladies, gentlemen, and gentlewomen, of divers counties, to the number of fourteen or fifteen hundred, and in general estimation about a hundred and fifty or more priests, most of them well known what they are."—*State Record Papers*, case 1, vol. cli., No. 13.

This is evidently from an informer, who perhaps exaggerates the number of priests.

The letter of Sir John Brydgeman, Sheriff of Shropshire, is as follows, dated A.D. 1636:

"To the Right Honourable the Lords of his Majesty's Most Honourable Privy Council, concerning Pilgrimages to Holywell.

"I have written to the Justices of the Peace next adjoining the Wells:

" 1st. To suppress all unnecessary alehouses;

" 2nd. To bind all innkeepers, etc., to take certain notice of such as shall resort there;

" 3rd. That they cause watches to be kept during the usual times of repair to the Well, which are in spring and summer. Which is as much as I conceive can be done for the present, until I may repair thither myself, which I propose (God willing) to do the week after Easter next, and to view the place, and to take the best course I may, either by *muring up the head* of the spring, where the superstition, as I am informed is used, or otherwise, by all the good means I can, to accomplish his Majesty's most gracious commands, and I humbly rest at your lordships' commandment.

"JOHN BRYDGEMAN.

" Ludlow, 3rd February, 1636."

These papers prove how great the devotion of the old Catholics of England was to the well. The public-houses in those times were not unfrequently kept by priests as innkeepers, or at least with a priest resident at or near them. The Cross Keys was one of these houses, situated where the present convent stands, with the hospice below; and another house stood on the site of the present priest's house and chapel.

The beautiful structure over the well was built by Margaret, Countess of Derby, the mother of Henry VII. The chapel above the well, which is part of it, was made a lumber-room at the Reformation, and again restored and fitted up for Mass by the Queen of James II., who gave for the purpose a donation of one hundred and forty crowns. The grant is signed "Mary Regina, Whitehall, A.D. 1687."

The chapel thus restored was given by the queen to a Father Thomas, who seems to have been of the Society of Jesus.

At the accession of William III. it again became a lumber-room, and is now used for a parish school. The beautiful groined roof below was hung until lately with the crutches of paralytics who had been cured in the Well.

CHAPTER X.

LATER MIRACLES.

ONE of the most celebrated miracles after the time of the Reformation, is the cure of the leprosy of Sir Roger Bodenham, in the year 1606. He was not a Catholic, but had an able physician, Dr. David Rees, a Catholic, who had professed physic at Padua. By his advice, after every remedy had been tried both by medicine and drinking waters at foreign medicinal springs, and all in vain, he undertook a journey to Holywell, bathed in the Well of St. Wenefred and was cured. He became a Catholic in consequence, and is the ancestor of the Bodenhams of Rotherwas, ever since faithful to the ancient creed.

Another very remarkable miracle took place, A.D. 1637. Mrs. Jane Wakeman of Rougeley, near Horsham in Sussex, had a cancer in the breast which was incurable. Accompanied by her husband and his brother, and a third witness who went with them, she passed through London to Beely in Worcestershire, where she left off all salves and applications to the wound, except a little linen to stanch it. At the first bath in the well the sore healed. She stayed but one night in Holywell, but made three visits to the well. She never afterwards had any pain or uneasiness in her breast.

Her husband, Mr. Richard Wakeman, in the signed document he left of her cure, attests that he saw a man lying dead by the side of the well. He had openly scoffed at St. Wenefred, and abused the pilgrims. The coroner was called to sit upon the body, and a jury impanelled. The verdict pronounced was that " God's just judgment was the cause of his death, for uncivil carriage in that place."

The year previous a bigot had ordered the image of St. Wenefred to be defaced, and some iron bars which supported bathers in the stream to be taken away. Both he and the men who executed his orders were punished not long after by extraordinary disasters which befell them.

In the year 1647, a singular miracle occurred of a person cured at a distance, by an act of devotion. The wife of a gardener at Worcester, a Mrs. John Cleck, went on a pilgrimage to Holywell for her health. On her way she passed through the town of Kidderminster, and called at the house of one Cooke, her cousin. In his house lay a bedridden woman put upon him as a householder by the parish, to be maintained as a pauper on parish relief. This poor woman overheard Mrs. Cleck saying that she was on a pilgrimage to Holywell, upon which she begged her to take a penny and bestow it as alms at the well upon some pilgrim there, asking his prayers. Mrs. Cleck did so, and upon her return found that at the very hour and day when she gave the penny at the well, the poor bedridden woman rose from her bed and walked. This miracle was attested by Mr. James Bridges, the sheriff of Worcester, the same who proclaimed King Charles in the year 1651.

To pass over many others, in the year 1666 a child of eight years old was carried under the great mill-wheel unhurt, though there were but two inches between the pavement and the wheel.

In 1673 a crippled boy from Cardiganshire, carried from hand to hand on a handbarrow the distance of ninety miles out of pity for his case, being put into the water of the well on the eleventh day of June, walked out of it perfectly cured.

In 1667, Roger Whetstone, a Quaker of Bromsgrove, in Worcestershire, came on crutches to Holywell. He could not be induced to bathe in the well as savouring of superstition and popery. But he drank a cup of the water, and fell into a trance. As soon as he came to himself he asked for another cup of the water, and having drank it, burst into tears for joy and threw away his crutches. He received baptism with his son eleven years of age, and some of the first people of the neighbourhood stood sponsors. This miracle is formally attested by Robert Hill, a rigid Quaker, the overseer of the poor of the parish of Bromsgrove.

The cure of Wenefred White, examined and attested by the saintly Dr. Milner, is another most authentic and indisputable miracle. The witnesses of it were people of different religions, conditions of life, and places of residence. She suffered from an incurable disease of the spine of a most painful nature, which rendered her incapable of work, and at times of movement for three years. Being conveyed to Holywell, at the first bath in the well on the 28th of June, she was perfectly freed from her malady and all pain. This occurred in the year 1805, and she afterwards was mistress of the Catholic poor school in Wolverhampton, the residence of Dr. Milner.

Thus for twelve hundred years there has been an uninterrupted succession of miracles at the well. Many of these are of an astonishing character, leaving no room for cavillers to say that it is the effect of some salubrious waters. Medicinal waters cannot make the stone-blind see, nor convert infidels. Moreover no one attributes any special medicinal quality to the water of the well.

The time is in a great measure past when it was the fashion to doubt of everything miraculous. There is a reaction and a craving in some minds for the preternatural; without the Catholic faith it degenerates into superstition, but where the mind is illumined by the true light of faith, superstition is eliminated. It is next to impossible for a true Catholic to be superstitious in the bad sense of the word. The firm belief in God, Holy Church, saints and relics, holy angels, sacraments and sacramental rites, give scope enough for what is implanted in every man, the sense and apprehension of an unseen world. Its legitimate satisfaction is the belief in the power of the Almighty, and in what He has revealed through His appointed teachers. Its unlawful satisfaction is belief in curious and mysterious arts and observations with which unsettled minds love to tamper, and in which heathens dealt of old, and which idolatrous nations still practise. It cannot be unlawful for a Christian to make use of things which the Church has by long use sanctioned, or the voice of its pontiffs proclaimed as good and salutary. It cannot be superstition to have recourse to a saint acknowledged by the Church as such to obtain relief, when such relief redounds to the glory of God and the honour of His saints. They are dear to Him as the apple of the eye. He who touches them touches His anointed, and in honouring them honours Him. The distinction between the pagan and the African who worships his obi, and the Christian who seeks in simplicity the help of God through his glorious saints, is as wide as that between man and the ape. The Christian acts reasonably—there are grounds of assurance that justify his act. The pagan acts from superstitious fears that have no real ground. The Christian acts from faith in the Incarnation, the heathen in the dread of imaginative apprehensions. The Christian loves and confides, the heathen and the infidel fears and crouches—these are the acts of an animal, and the worship implied is bestial. The simplicity of the Catholic who believes when he gathers a faded flower from the bier of a saint, or moss from St. Wenefred's Well, is agreeable to the great God, the Father of All, because it implies a belief in that Goodness which loves to communicate to chosen creatures its own divine gifts, and pour forth blessings on those who seek Him.

CHAPTER XI.

THE WELL AT THE PRESENT DAY.

AT the present day, as every priest who has had the privilege of serving the mission at Holywell can attest, miracles are of constant occurrence. Conversions are made of Protestants, who have come for cures on hearsay of the wonders wrought there. The blind recover their sight, as in the case of the soldier examined before the county magistrate, Lord Denbigh, the father of the present earl. The man had lost his eyes in Egypt, and for years had been led by a boy. He recovered his sight at the well.

Many of these miracles of the present times were recorded by the late Father Maurice Mann, missioner for some years at Holywell, and the author himself can attest that in the space of three weeks he was witness to the cure and conversion of a Protestant, the wonderful restoration of a paralysed Catholic, from whose shoulders the steam was seen to rise out of the cold bath as if from boiling water at the moment of his cure, and the recovery of a poor creature almost demented from religious monomania.

There is now an almshouse or hospitium, built for the reception of poor pilgrims by the exertions of Father Maurice Mann. Pope Pius IX. sent his blessing to the work, and indulgences are attached to visits to the chapel of St. Wenefred and the well.

The well itself is a wonder, producing every minute a hundred tons of water. It never freezes, and seldom varies in quantity either in the greatest droughts or after the heaviest rains. The water is pure and sweet, the moss on the sides of the well fragrant. The stone of St. Beuno is in the outer basin, where bathers usually enter the water. The inner well is a burst of heaving water, rushing up with such force and impetuosity that no one could descend into it.

In conclusion, we add the Litany of St. Wenefred :

Lord have mercy upon us.
Christ have mercy upon us.
Lord have mercy upon us.
God the Father of Heaven, have mercy upon us.
God the Son, Redeemer of mankind, have mercy upon us.
God the Holy Ghost, have mercy upon us.
Holy Trinity, One God, have mercy upon us

Holy Mary, pray for us.
Holy Mother of God,
Holy Virgin of Virgins,
Blessed St. Wenefride,
Virgin humble and meek,
Glorious Spouse of Christ,
Virgin most kind and charitable,
Sweet comforter of the afflicted,
Singular example of chastity,
Shining star,
Flower of all Britain,
Admirable vessel of election,
Mirror of chastity,
Mirror of piety and devotion,
Bright lamp of sanctity,
Golden image of angelic purity,
Hope and help of pilgrims in distress, pray for us,
That we may be delivered from all iniquity,
That we may be delivered from all disorders of the mind,
That we may be delivered from the deceits of the world, the flesh, and the devil,
That we may be delivered from all occasions of sin,
That we may be delivered from all plague, famine, and war,
That we may be delivered from the wrath of God and eternal damnation,
That we and all sinners may have true contrition and full remission of our sins,
That all schismatics, heretics, and infidels may be converted to the holy Catholic and Apostolical faith,
That we may always hate sin and overcome all temptation,
That we may despise all worldly vanities and delights,
That we may ever fear God and fulfil His holy Will,
That we may have both spiritual and corporal health,
That we may devoutly affect chastity and purity of life,

The Well at the Present Day.

That we may fervently love humility and meekness,
That we may delight in pious prayers, fasting, and charitable alms,
That we may discreetly and fervently continue in the exercise of godliness,
That we may cheerfully and constantly suffer for the love of Christ,
That the souls in purgatory and all afflicted persons may obtain heavenly consolation,
That our benefactors and all that labour to save souls may be blest with abundance of grace and everlasting life,
That we may enjoy true peace and endless felicity,
That God of His abundant mercy may vouchsafe to bless this our pilgrimage,
That by thy pious intercession it may be the perfect health of our souls and bodies,
That thou wilt vouchsafe to grant our requests, O Blessed Wenefride,

Holy Virgin and Martyr, pray for us.

Let us pray.

Almighty and everlasting God, who hast adorned St. Wenefride with the reward of virginity, grant us, we beseech Thee, by her pious intercession, to set aside the delights of the world, and obtain with her the throne of everlasting glory. Through Jesus Christ our Lord. Amen.

Another Prayer.

Almighty and everlasting God, we humbly beseech Thee that Blessed Wenefride may obtain for us such spiritual and temporal benefits as are expedient for Thy holy service and our eternal salvation, through Jesus Christ our Lord. Amen.

CHAPTER XII.

APPENDIX.

No. I.

THE received tradition of Joseph of Arimathea has been given in the first chapter. It is supported by the fact that it was received at councils out of Britain to substantiate the claim of English bishops to precedence in place. It was acknowledged through the Saxon and Norman times down to the Reformation, and fought for by the Reformers themselves as a plea against the priority of the preaching of St. Peter in Britain. Parker uses the argument, poor as it is, because the coming of St. Joseph to the far west was subsequent to the probable date of St. Peter's coming to the far ends of the world and Britain spoken of by a Greek historian.

The grandeur of Glastonbury, enriched as it was from the very first by British donations, then by Saxon, may be guessed from the ruins

Appendix. 73

of the church, five hundred feet in length. The list of great saints buried there is given in the Chronicle of John of Glastonbury. The finding of Arthur's tomb is given by Alford, in his Chronicles, or Annals of the Church in England. From Glastonbury came the monks who were sent by King Lucius to Pope Eleutherius, to ask for missionaries to convert Britain. The great St. Dunstan was educated and was abbot there. Its magnificence is attested by the beautiful remains of the chapel of St. Joseph. The flowering thorn, cut down by a Puritan to put an end to Popish miracles, still blossoms at Christmas and again in spring. For the above facts, and the many gifts of land made by the Saxon kings to Glastonbury, see Alford's Annals, *passim*, tom. i. and ii.

No. II.

THE existence of Arthur has been questioned by modern incredulity. So has the reality of such personages as Romulus and Remus, and of Agamemnon. The tombs of the kings of Mycenæ, lately opened, attest the existence of the old Grecian heroes. To those who sneer at the name of Arthur as historical, let Gibbon answer, who, in chapter xxxviii. of "The Decline and Fall," says:

"Every British name is effaced by the illustrious name of Arthur, the hereditary prince of the Silures in South Wales, and elective king or general of the nation. According to the most rational account he defeated in twelve successive battles the Angles of the north and the Saxons of the south.

"During a period of five hundred years the tradition of his exploits was preserved by the obscure bards of Wales and Armorica, who were odious to the Saxons and unknown to the rest of mankind. The pride and curiosity of the Norman conquerors prompted them to inquire into the ancient history of Britain. They listened with fond credulity to the tale of Arthur, and eagerly applauded the merit of a prince who had triumphed over the Saxons, their common enemies.

"The gallantry and superstition of the British hero, his feasts and tournaments, and the honourable institution of his 'Round Table,' were faithfully copied from the reigning manners of chivalry and the fabulous exploits of Uther's son, appear less incredible than the adventures which were achieved by the enterprising valour of the Normans.

"At length the visionary fable melted into air, and by a natural, though *unjust, reverse* of the public opinion, the *severity* of the present age is *inclined to question the existence* of Arthur."

In a note Mr. Gibbon says: "As I am a stranger to the Welsh bards, Myrddin, Llomach, and Taliessin, my faith in the existence and exploits of Arthur principally rests on the simple and circumstantial testimony of Nennius. Mr. Whitaker has framed an interesting and even [probable narrative of the wars of Arthur."

John, the Chronicler of Glastonbury, gives the pedigree of Arthur on the mother's side: "Arthur, son of Uther and Ygern, daughter of Lambord's son. Lambord, son of Manael, son of Castellon, son of Aminadab, son of Josue, son of Helains, nephew of Joseph of Arimathea" (*De rebus Glastoniensibus: Brit. Mus.*).

No. III.

IT is a common topic of Protestant writers to allege that the British Church was not Roman Catholic because it did not surrender its independence to St. Augustine. He was commissioned by the Pope to preach to the English, and had no mission to the British as such, who were already Christians. His overtures were made to them to join in the work of evangelising the Saxon. This they rejected, as well as submission to him as their archbishop. They had their own in the successor of St. David, who was in an especial manner a true maintainer of the Catholic Faith and of union with the See of Rome. It is not necessary to repeat here what has been shown in the "Life of St. Willibrord," that the question on the keeping of Easter and other frivolous alleged differences of the British Church from Catholic practices, form no real grounds for argument that the Celtic Christianity was anti-Roman or anti-Catholic. As has been observed in the " Life of St. Wenefred," the very fact of the proposition that the British clergy should join in the conversion of the Saxon proves that St. Augustine considered them orthodox in their teaching.

The objection made to the truth of the life of St. Wenefred because it is ignored by St. Bede is equally absurd. Wales was as much cut off from the knowledge of Bede, who professed only to chronicle the history of the Saxons, as any foreign land. Neither the language nor the people were known at Jarrow, except as bitter, implacable foes of Northumbria, allies of Panda, the ruthless and heathen king of Mercia. Bede had no means of communication with the inhabitants of Gwynedd and Powysland. It even took ages for the Saxons to learn something of the saints of Wales. The translation of St. Wenefred to Shrewsbury drew their attention to her history, but it was not until the year 1420 that Henry, the Archbishop of Canterbury, in a provincial synod, appointed the feast of St. Wenefred to be solemnly kept all over England with an office of nine lessons on the 3rd of November (*Lindewode*, fol. 70).

Incidentally in Bede there is great notice of Celtic sanctity when interwoven with the history of the Saxons. St. Aidan and all his school of Columkill, Mailros, and Lindisfarne, belong to Celtic glory. The great British Church, with its three archbishops and thirty bishops, had been swept away from England, and the Saxons were not disposed to inquire into the forgotten glories of their hereditary foes.

No. IV.

ST. DEIFER—in Welsh—Diheufar, was son of Aristobulus the Lame, in Welsh, Arwystli Gloff—so called to distinguish him from Aristobulus the Old, Arwystli Hên—a "disciple," says Cressy, of Sts. Peter and Paul, first bishop of Britain, who died in Glastonbury, A.D. 99. Aristobulus the Lame married Tywynneth, daughter of Amlawdd, the chief commander or Gwledig, and had four sons, Sts. Tyfrydog, Twrnog, Tudyr, and Deifer, and a daughter, St. Marcella.

This Aristobulus was the youngest son of Seithenin or Sennan. His brothers were St. Gwynnodd, St. Merin or Gwytherin, St. Senefyr, St. Tudglyd, St. Tudno, St. Tyneio or Deneio. Thus St. Deifer numbered three brothers and a sister, and six uncles, saints.

Aristobulus or Arwystli retired in his old age to the holy isle of Bardsey, Inys Enlli; all his brothers were inmates of the Monastery of Bangor Iscoed. The Monastery of Bardsey was founded by St. Cadwan from Armorica and the king Einion—Einion Frenhin. The "blessed land of Enlli," or Bardsey Isle, lies off the western promontory of Carnarvonshire. According to Pennant, it is about three leagues from the mainland, between which and the isle there flows a rapid current. It is called Inys Enlli from this current of the sea, and the passage is accounted dangerous. Its narrow limits, scarcely exceeding three miles in circumference, are said, according to Rees (pp. 213, 214), to enclose the bodies of twenty thousand saints. St. Dubricius retired there to end his days, and pilgrimages were made to it. Even in Pennant's time, in the latter portion of the last century, the boatmen, as they approached it, pulled off their hats and offered a short prayer. The abbey was dedicated to the Blessed Virgin.

St. Deifer, by his prayers, raised a well at Bodvari, as Robert of Salop relates in the life of St. Wenefred. It was celebrated for miraculous cures, and a processional service was long kept up at the well on Ascension Day. Isaac Maddox, Bishop of St. Asaph A.D. 1736—43, says that in his time they went in procession on Ascension Day to read the Litany, Ten Commandments, Epistle, and Gospel. He then relates that superstitious practices are customary there, as is often the case when true religion has left some memory to a spot—namely, the offering of chicken by the poorest person in the parish after going nine times round the well, a cockerel for a boy, and a pullet for a girl. Children also are dipped to the neck at the three corners of the well, to prevent their crying by night.—*Bp. Maddox; MS. Bk.*

THE END.

www.ingramcontent.com/pod-product-compliance
Lightning Source LLC
Chambersburg PA
CBHW020325090426
42735CB00009B/1406